PREHIS
CAMBRIDG

LINT   2/24   donation

ALISON TAYLOR

THE   DGE

The Oleander Press
17 Stansgate Avenue
Cambridge CB2 2QZ

ISBN 0 900891 05 X

Cover illustration:
Bronze Age equipment

Title page illustration:
Iron Age fire-dog from Barton
(photo E. Taylor)

Designed by Ron Jones

Printed and bound by The Burlington Press, Foxton.

PREHISTORIC CAMBRIDGESHIRE

Introduction

Local archaeology is a new subject to most people, and yet of all studies it must have the closest connections with everyday life and our own locality. Our ancestors who brought agriculture, house-building, metal-working, social organisation, warfare and religion to Cambridgeshire are all part of our background just as much as the colourful named figures of national history, and the ways they made their living and organised their lives, reacting to certain elements in the environment and leaving their mark on others, has an abiding fascination. Those who want to take a critical look at our own society's place in history in particular need this sort of perspective and we are fortunate that Cambridgeshire has such an honourable history in archaeo-logical studies and we can therefore present so much material to the modern reader.

This present series of four booklets on Cambridgeshire history will look at the current state of knowledge regarding man's development in the County from Palaeolithic times to around 1500 AD. In this prehistoric section we are dependent on archaeology in the strictest sense of the word as it relates to the physical remains of human activity generally found beneath the soil, although the accounts of Roman, Anglo-Saxon and Mediaeval Cambridgeshire will be able to use historical and literary sources. It seemed necessary to include brief descriptions of the major sources of our information, for with-out knowing such background and limitations it is not really possible to understand the problems of prehistory or prehistorians. It also seemed sensible to include enough background information on each period for general readers to be able to relate local sites to national developments, but of course this information has to be in a very abbreviated form and those who become more deeply interested will find no shortage of suitable works in local book-shops and libraries. As far as details of particular excavations are concerned, most of these are published in journals such as the *Proceedings* of the Cambridge Antiquarian Society, and references in full will be given at the end.

3

Geographical Background

Before we can start to look at the archaeological details of early settlement we should note the physical aspects of Cambridgeshire that still affect our patterns of settlement and land-use to-day and would have meant prosperity or starvation to the hunters and farmers living here in prehistoric times. This account therefore starts with the natural regions of Cambridgeshire, the effects of geography and geology and the impact of the landscape on man.

The geographical setting of Cambridgeshire near the East Coast with access to the sea via the Wash affected the influences entering the County throughout prehistory, for there was a comparatively easy sea-route to Northern England and Europe which was evidently used for trade and immigration. At the same time the south of the County is on the line of the Icknield Way, an open tract of passable countryside linking Wiltshire to Norfolk and providing cultural and trading contacts all along its route, and so there were influences from Southern England.

Other natural transport systems linking prehistoric settlers were the rivers Welland, Nene, Ouse and Cam, and the waterways of the Fens. Hollowed out canoes were in use at least from the Neolithic period, and all the rivers were navigable, providing much easier passage than most of the possible overland routes through the wooded landscape.

The main effect of geology on prehistoric man was the limitation imposed by the shortage of suitable land for primitive agriculture. The evidence at present available suggests that the heavy clay lands were too difficult to clear and plough and our distribution maps at present show very little habitation in these areas. The chalk lands were generally too dry for settlement except along the spring line, but the presence of the Icknield Way led to the deposition of many Bronze Age hoards by travelling smiths who never recovered them, and a number of burial mounds were sited near the route.

Alluvial gravels along the river valleys would be the most accessible regions, less heavily wooded and easier to cultivate than clay soils, while the rivers themselves provided abundant water, fishing and transport. It is not surprising, therefore, that we see much greater concentrations of prehistoric sites along the river valleys than in most other areas.

The Fens must be one of the few areas of the world whose actual geographical setting has changed significantly in the last two thousand years, for the silting up of land between the medieval sea-bank and the Wash means Cambridgeshire no longer has the stretch of sea-coast which reached to Wisbech; variations in sea-level and climate and artificial drainage have led to a series of major changes in possible land-uses; and even the rivers on the seaward side of Cambridge and Earith have changed from prehistoric and Roman times.

Relative height of land above sea-level was the main factor affecting settlement in the Fens for very slight changes can cause an area to be water-logged or fertile soil. In Mesolithic times, it seems the Fens were about thirty feet higher than at present, and therefore offered wide expanses of country-side that was only lightly wooded and well provided with lakes and streams. In Neolithic and Bronze Age times, about 3,000 - 650 BC, land levels were about fifteen feet lower, but still the slightly higher parts, particularly on and around the islands and near the fen-edge, were evidently heavily settled. It is easy to see why this should be the case when we remember the traditional advantages of the Fens which were exploited in the Middle Ages, including fish, eels, fowl, turves, reeds, willows and summer pasture for cattle. People living within reach of both upland where they could live and farm and the fenland could live very comfortably, and land in such areas was exploited to the full. Only in the Iron Age, about 650 BC - 43 AD, does there seem to be climatic decline and a retreat to higher ground, although a number of settlements can be proven even then.

Another geological factor affecting man and his archaeology is the availability of natural building materials. Only in the limestone districts near Peterborough is there good building stone, and in some other areas such as fens and chalklands even suitable timber might be scarce. The most common building material was wattle and daub around a framework of stakes, and we assume that roofs were generally straw or reed thatch. Clay bat (unbaked mud bricks) and clunch (an unusually hard kind of chalk) which we know were used in Roman and mediaeval times might also have occurred in pre-historic dwellings but so far there is no evidence for this.

In practical terms of local archaeology the impact of modern man on the landscape is also very significant for it affects both the discovery and survival of our basic data. Agriculture is one important factor, for ploughing erodes earthwork sites while at the same time making it possible for stray finds to be turned up and reported and also, where an arable crop is grown, for crop-marks to be photographed. Land which is predominantly pasture, usually on clay soils, will preserve the earthworks created by the latest phases of occupation. These earthworks have great value to the archaeologist because they are the most complete sites we can normally find.

Later settlement will also make it more difficult to recognise early sites although it will not necessarily obliterate every trace. This makes the problem of how much continuity of settlement there was in a given area difficult to resolve and probably hides a number of important sites which are likely to be situated on the areas most favoured for settlement to-day.

Discovery of sites

One of the obvious problems facing archaeologists is to tell where a site exists and what is its importance before excavation or destruction takes place. This is vital for plotting settlement patterns, protecting the most significant sites and planning excavations where they are most needed. There are no infallible sources but most of the evidence we are gathering to-day about prehistoric sites comes from aerial photographs, earthworks, field-walking and chance finds.

Aerial photographs

More new sites have been discovered by aerial photography than by any other technique and its development over the last thirty years has drastically affected our ideas concerning population density and distribution. The nature of our sites has also changed, for previously they had to be substantial standing monuments of earth or stone, or else provide rich scatters of easily recognised artifacts if they were likely to be recognised before disturbance, whereas now farming settlements with ditches, pits and trackways are most likely to be noted.

The reason why crop-marks occur is that the growth and ripening of grain-crops are affected by soil conditions and these in turn can be locally affected by archaeological features. A stone wall or metalled road a few inches below the surface, for example, will lead to a parching of the crop as soon as there is any water-shortage, and will in any case cause stunted growth and limited foliage. Conversely, and more commonly, a pit or ditch with humus-rich fill cut into a porous sub-soil such as chalk or gravel will retain moisture and produce a lusher crop than the surrounding field. It is likely also to ripen more slowly and may therefore be a different colour at certain stages. Heavy soils, such as clay, retain water better and crop-marks are much less likely to occur. In extreme conditions grass and other vegetation such as sugar-beet will show differential growth, but normally clear marks only show in grain-crops. These crop-marks will sometimes be visible on the ground but they can hardly be recorded there when in a field of growing corn, and much the easiest way to see and photograph a complex of marks is from a low-flying aircraft.

Similar aerial photographs are also the best way to record sites showing as soil-marks, which occur when the dark humic fill of archaeological features shows up against a light subsoil such as chalk when it is freshly ploughed. Slight earthworks which appear as random irregularities to someone standing on the ground, also give a clearer picture on an aerial photograph, especially if taken with a low evening or early morning sun which casts long shadows.

Earthwork sites

Earthworks were sometimes created when earth was thrown up deliberately to create memorial or defensive structures or they might occur accidentally due to activities such as house-buildings, mining or agriculture. These accidental

1. Crop-marks of an Iron Age and Roman settlement at Great Shelford, excavated 1975-6
(© by kind permission of the Cambridge University Aerial Photography Department)

causes have left many important sites in later periods, but in Cambridgeshire the only prehistoric earthworks so far identified are round-barrows, which were used for burials mostly in the Bronze Age but sometimes also in Iron Age and Roman times, and Iron Age forts such as Stonea and Wandlebury. In neighbouring counties long barrows of Neolithic date survive, but none of these have so far been identified in Cambridgeshire.

Field Walking

If ploughed fields are systematically walked by archaeologists who collect everything of possible archaeological interest such as flint flakes, fire-cracked stones, pottery and metal fragments, and the occurrence and relative density of such occupation debris is plotted, then new sites can often be discovered and more information can be deduced from those already known.

Chance finds

Extensive earth disturbance may be the despair of the archaeologist, but it is unfortunately true that without it the subject would probably not exist and we would lack most of our spectacular objects. Most of our local finds came to light during ploughing, peat cutting, coprolite and gravel quarrying and the construction of new buildings, canals and railways, and we are still very reliant on finders showing objects to museums and stating exactly where they were found.

Palaeolithic Cambridgeshire c.40,000 - c.7,500 BC

For this vast span of years while the world was becoming habitable and man was evolving into his modern form, we have to rely on rare sites in abnormal states of preservation for any real indication of his economy, culture and even physical characteristics. We assume a hunting economy, mostly dependent on big-game, with small groups that moved constantly and had discovered the use of fire, made clothes and tents from skins, and chipped flints into tools such as hand-axes which sometimes attained quite elegant forms.

Our knowledge of Cambridgeshire in this period depends on a great number of hand-axes and other stone tools, all too often found by chance in gravel-pits and with no possibility of noticing their context and less spectacular but informative associated finds. Only occasionally can flint-working sites be identified but quite good examples have been studied at Woodston, St Neots, Swaffham Prior and Allington Hill.[1] Most tools have been found in river valleys at some distance from the sea. There are heavy concentrations around the Nene at Peterborough and the Cam at Cambridge, most notably from the Travellers Rest Pit near the A45.[2]

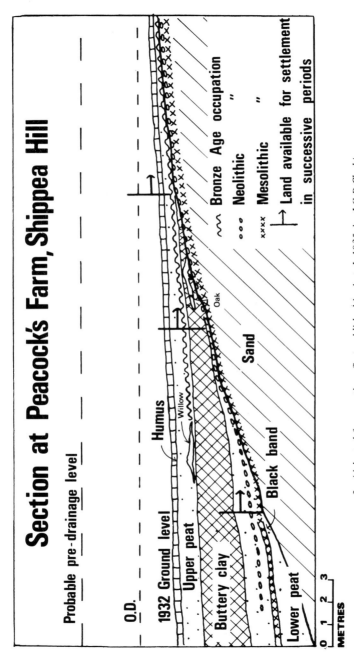

Section at Peacock's Farm, Shippea Hill

Probable pre-drainage level

O.D.

1932 Ground level

Humus

Willow

Upper peat

Buttery clay

Oak

Black band

Sand

Lower peat

0 1 2 3
METRES

∿∿∿ Bronze Age occupation

ₒₒₒ Neolithic "

xxxx Mesolithic "

↑ Land available for settlement in successive periods

2. (Adapted from sections first published in Ant. J. 1935, by J G D Clark)

Mesolithic Cambridgeshire c.7,500 - c.3,000 BC

During this period sea levels rose and the English Channel and the North Sea cut Britain off from easy contacts with the Continent. Climatic changes brought to an end the big-game hunting economy of the Palaeolithic and forced the population to an apparently poorer but technically more advanced subsistence economy; they hunted with bows and arrows, fished with harpoons, and made composite tools with skilfully shaped microliths gummed into wooden handles.

In Cambridgeshire the characteristic Mesolithic worked flints, which are normally the only sign remaining by which we can trace settlement patterns, tend to be found on patches of sandy heath land, such as areas near Gamlingay.

The Fenlands are particularly interesting during this period for we have to imagine a landscape completely different from the traditional picture of undrained fenland which belongs to later times. As the Fens were about thirty feet higher in relation to sea levels than they are now, the peat and silt had scarcely started to form in the deepest parts, and slightly higher ground was dry and open, providing excellent sites for habitation in contrast to the inhospitable wooded landscape of upland areas.

It was in 1932-4 that J G D Clark and H Godwin excavated at Shippea Hill.[3] They dug through Bronze Age, Neolithic and Mesolithic layers and were able to find sufficient occupation debris to date the formation of different layers of peat and buttery clay and to demonstrate which areas were available for habitation at successive dates. Their results are summarized by the section reproduced below, which was first published in 1938 and which remains the clearest explanation we have of the formation and prehistoric settlement of the Fens. H Godwin analysed the pollen that was preserved in this and nearby sites, and so was able to catalogue the changing vegetation of the Fenlands.

Neolithic Cambridgeshire c.3,000 - c.1,800 BC

The technical improvements that distinguish this age from the preceding Mesolithic, such as the invention of pottery and new techniques of stone-working, are a godsend to archaeologists but need not in themselves have much affected the life-style of the people. It is the economic revolution of the beginnings of agriculture that makes the Neolithic the most significant period of prehistory and which in the course of time led to all the advances made possible by social stability and modest prosperity. For the first time Man could influence the environment for his own ends and could make impressions on the landscape still detectable to-day.

The first farmers have been recognised in the Near East around 8,000 BC,

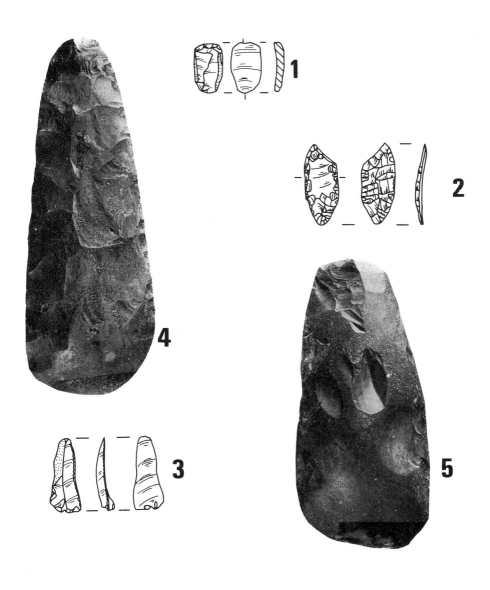

3. Neolithic tools. Two chipped and ground flint axes from Shelford, and worked flints from Fengate *(Drawn by F Pryor in Durobrivae I)* (Lengths — 1.=5 cms, 2.= 9 cms, 3.=8 cms, 4.=16 cms, 5.=12.5 cms)

when quite large settled groups domesticated the grains and animals that occurred naturally in their homelands, made pottery and engaged in trade. It was probably due to population pressures, which naturally made good hunting scarcer than ever, that more people were willing to learn farming skills and accustom themselves to the ceaseless labour and precarious returns of prehistoric farming. The easiest agriculture was 'slash and burn' whereby natural woodland was burnt down and the soil worked until it lost its fertility. The band of farmers would then move to a fresh area, and so Neolithic agriculture and other skills spread slowly across Europe, entering Britain about 3,000 BC.

The visible effects of Neolithic activity on the archaeological record in Britain are long barrows covering the burials of family groups, ritual monuments and ceremonial meeting places known as henges and causewayed camps and hut-sites which are detectable only during scientific excavations. These all point to an orderly people who honoured dead relatives and whatever gods they worshipped with substantial monuments, would work together in large numbers for some common aim, and had some surplus produce.

Settlements

Unfortunately, the archaeology of Neolithic Cambridgeshire has suffered so much from the plough that we have not a single site that exists as a standing monument, and all our knowledge of the period depends on crop mark sites, chance finds and concentrations of flint tools and waste flakes. Fortunately, the picture we are given is remarkably consistent and in fact agrees with the pattern one would expect from people in a wooded landscape who had only stone tools to clear and till the ground, whose agriculture was precarious and would naturally be augmented by hunting and fishing and whose transport could be either by boat or on foot. A good supply of fresh water was of course one essential for any habitation site, as it was to remain until very recent times.

It is therefore not surprising to find that the thickly-wooded heavy clay soils to the west and south-east of the County were generally avoided and that nearly all sites are found along the light gravel soils of the river valleys and on the fen islands, especially Whittlesey, Manea and Ely. The greatest density of all is along the edge of the Fens, right round from Burwell and Wicken to Fengate.

Fengate, near Peterborough, is probably the richest multi-period site in Eastern England. The site has been known to be of vital archaeological importance since 1908 when the local antiquary, G Wyman-Abbott, watched gravel-diggings in the area and recovered large collections of prehistoric objects. When the area became designated for industrial development as part of Peterborough New Town it was realised that large-scale archaeological

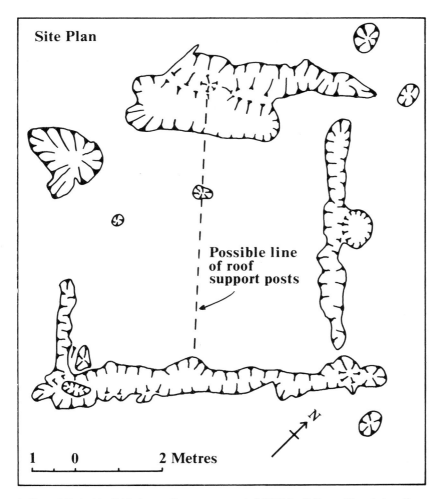

Site Plan

Possible line
of roof
support posts

N

1   0   2 Metres

4. Plan of Early Neolithic hut at Fengate, excavated 1972 by F Pryor *(Durobrivae I)*

action was needed, and so in 1972 Francis Pryor began an annual series of excavations, financed by the Royal Ontario Museum and the Nene Valley Research Committee.

In the first year the foundation trenches of a small hut about seven metres square were discovered. Radiocarbon dating on the site put this house at about 3,000 BC, which means it is the earliest known in lowland England. In spite of the large areas cleared archaeologically since then no more Neolithic huts have turned up, and it seems that this very early phase consisted of one pioneer family.[4]

By a remarkable coincidence, three years after the discovery of the hut the excavations at Fengate uncovered a group of skeletons which, as far as can be judged by the dating methods at an archaeologist's disposal, could be contemporary with the hut and therefore are likely to be some of the inhabitants. The bodies all lay in one grave-pit and included a man of about thirty, crouched on his right side, and at his feet lay a small child and the remains of two adults who had been pushed aside to make room for him. It was the crouched male whose death produced the essential evidence for dating this group, for between his ribs was found a leaf-shaped arrowhead, distinctive enough in style to be dated to around 3,000 BC. The skeletons, with the arrow-head still in position, were lifted intact in a block of earth and are now on display in Peterborough Museum. Incidentally, this find also gives evidence which we would not otherwise suspect at this date of the tensions which already existed in a totally rural, non-hierarchical and thinly populated society where there were no shortages of food or land and very few goods worth stealing.

It was about a thousand years later, but still in the same Neolithic period, about 2,000 BC, that the archaeological record at Fengate shows a great increase in population and a pattern of fields was laid out that lasted for about eight hundred years. The fields, which were obviously used for cattle and probably also small crops of grain were marked by ditches (and presumably, banks and hedges). They were straight-sided with corner entrance ways and there was one particularly narrow droveway, ditched on both sides so that cattle could only walk in single file, which Francis Pryor suggests was used to inspect or mark the animals.

The farm included a small well, at the bottom of which was preserved, thanks to the high water table at Fengate, a lining of woven twigs, and another deep waterlogged pit preserved a notched alder log that must have been used as a ladder.

The foundations of the actual houses inhabited while these fields were farmed were not discovered, but the main living area was identified by a concentration of household debris that was surrounded by a circular ditch. Within this ditch there were various hollows in which had accumulated the usual sort of archaeological "occupation debris" which survives so well — charcoal, pot fragments, animal bones, and flint tools and waste flakes.

The only other Neolithic house to be excavated so far in Cambridgeshire was found in circumstances very different from the carefully planned large-scale work at Fengate. In 1967 there was a road improvement scheme at Little Paxton on the A1, and when the topsoil was stripped off a number of archaeological features were exposed. Unfortunately there was only time for the archaeologist in charge, Granville Rudd, to fully examine one feature that

5. Excavations of the Neolithic farm at Fengate. Note the squared ditched field and (bottom right) part of the main dwelling area encircled by a deep ditch *(Excavation by F Pryor, photo and © Peterborough Standard)*

looked the most promising. This turned out to be a D-shaped hut with the straight side marked by post holes and the curved side bounded by an irregular trench filled with a very dark, slightly fibrous material probably turf. A cutting right across the hut showed that half the floor had been dug away about twelve to fifteen inches deep, leaving a raised bench about two feet wide along the straight side of the hut. The lower part of the floor seemed to be covered with straw, which the excavator thought might be a bed. There were six inches of soil over this straw, more straw on top of the soil, and finally a covering of soil over both the bed and bench areas.

The hut had evidently been built with turf walls on three sides, eighteen inches to two feet thick, supported by posts and stakes. There was an entrance on the straight side and two large posts supported the rest of this wall which was probably covered with boards or skins. Apparently there were rafters radiating from the posts sloping to the turf walls and fastened to the supporting stakes.[5]

The Economy
A man's livelihood in Cambridgeshire in the Neolithic period depended on simple subsistence farming based on cattle, pig, sheep, wheat and barley, but as the only real evidence consists of a few grain impressions that were accidentally burnt into pots during firing and animal bones from farmyard and household rubbish it is quite impossible to give any total picture of their agriculture. The only good scientific evidence we are likely to get in Cambridgeshire in the near future once again comes from Fengate, where the

15

results of total excavations of fields and habitation areas should soon give us some comprehensible statistics relating to that particular farm. This site is probably fairly typical of the numerous sites clustering around the edge of the Fens which were obviously deliberately sited to take advantage of two very different environments, fenland and upland, a pattern of settlement that lasted well into the Middle Ages.

The importance of this situation reminds us that the introduction of farming is most unlikely to have meant an end to the long Mesolithic tradition of hunting, fishing and gathering, which, after all, provided a living for some fenmen within living memory. Flint arrowheads are found quite commonly in all areas of Neolithic settlement and must have been the main hunting weapon (though of course a few might kill other men as in the Fengate example), and we should eventually expect to retrieve bird and fish bones from archaeological deposits by very careful sieving.

The only industries for which we are likely to find evidence are pottery and flint working. Pots were made by the coil method, sometimes decorated with convenient objects such as bird bones, twisted cord and finger nails, and fired to a soft fabric in bonfires. Possibly these pots were produced by a village potter but there is no reason why they should not have been made at home by their owners. The styles and decoration of these pots appear consistently over much of Britain, demonstrating that there were always certain "cultural connections" between the scattered farmsteads. We cannot assume there was trade in the modern sense of straight exchanges over long distances, involving specialized merchants, for there was more likely to be a transmission of ideas and fashions by inter-marriage, gifts (some, no doubt, extorted) and seasonal gatherings.

This sort of social exchange probably accounts for the occurrence of occasional more exotic items found in Cambridgeshire such as the three beautiful very highly polished axes from Histon, Cambridge and Burwell, now on display in the Museum of Archaeology and Ethnology, Cambridge, which are so slim that one cannot imagine they were ever used for chopping wood. Their origin is unknown but they are probably central European. A jet bead from Fengate must have originated in Yorkshire and there are numerous polished axes all over the county which come from Wales and Langdale Pike in the Lake District.

Flint working was doubtless a "cottage industry" with most individuals capable of chipping out the tools they needed, although perhaps there were recognized experts making the finer examples. The polished axes, especially, required a great deal of time consuming labour and were probably made on dark winter evenings when there was little else to do, although at Wilbraham there was a hoard of four chipped and partially polished axes, unused and found packed together which look like the hoard of a specialist stone-worker.

16

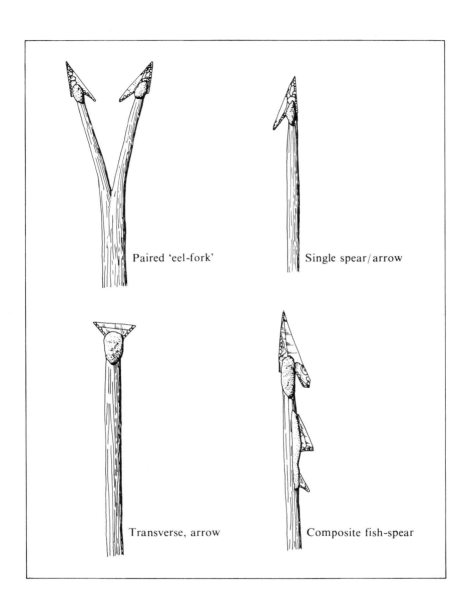

Paired 'eel-fork'

Single spear/arrow

Transverse, arrow

Composite fish-spear

6. Suggested methods of hafting arrow-heads found at Fengate *(F Pryor, in Durobrivae I)*

Not all areas, however, had suitable types of flint occurring naturally, so this would have to be collected from some neighbouring source, and it is clear from the flint that was used even in areas where it does occur that particular types, especially very black shiny flint would still be imported for tools in preference to the native resources. A famous source of high quality black flint was, of course, the flint mines of Grimes Graves, just over the border in Norfolk where highly developed mining techniques provided great quantities of flint nodules for export. One other item of interest regarding stone working was at Burwell where there was found a grinding slab of sandstone associated with two axes of flint and some fragments of greenstone suitable for making axes, suggesting that it was just the raw material that was normally imported and that the craftsmanship or at least the finishing stages of it was carried out locally.

Burials

So far no Neolithic burial sites have been discovered in Cambridgeshire, apart from the group in a pit at Fengate, already described. One can only say that if all other burials were like that, but without the arrow that was lodged in the man's ribs and therefore virtually undateable, it is not surprising no others have come to light. Normally one would expect burials in family groups beneath long barrows like the example on Royston Heath, but if any did exist they have now been ploughed away. The only possible examples of long barrows were at Buckworth, which have been trenched without any result, and which have now disappeared, and a cropmark that is the right shape for the quarry ditch around a long barrow at Swaffham Prior.

Ceremonial Sites

Religious sites that are known to be built in this period are henges, the most famous of which is the first phase of Stonehenge in Wiltshire. Elsewhere in Britain uprights were erected of wood, not stone, and so the only surviving archaeological remains are the holes where the posts stood, and the ditch enclosing the site. No such sites have been excavated in Cambridgeshire, but circular cropmarks at Elton, Melbourn and Wilbraham look very likely candidates. Stonehenge is either some sort of temple or an elaborate astronomical tool and perhaps the Cambridgeshire examples marked similar meeting places for festivals and ceremonies, but at the moment this is purely hypothetical.

Causewayed camps on high points, mostly in the south of England, consist of large enclosures surrounded by one or more circular ditches interrupted by entrance-ways. The excavations that have taken place on this sort of site seem to show that there was a certain amount of occupation near the ditches but not enough to suggest permanent settlement and it is thought they might be points for seasonal meetings, possibly involving the counting and exchange of cattle. The surrounding ditches are quite shallow and can never have served a defensive function, except against straying animals, and in places it looks as if they have been deliberately filled in at various stages in the Neolithic period, but why this should have happened we cannot say.

In Cambridgeshire such camps are found on low lying ground, usually near rivers, and as with nearly all of our prehistoric sites in Cambridgeshire, they have all been ploughed until they are quite flat and so they can only be identified from cropmarks. The two examples so far identified in Cambridgeshire are at Melbourn and Wilbraham, which is interesting in view of the three henges mentioned above. At Wilbraham in the autumns of 1975 and 1976 there have been short excavations organized by Cambridge University and the British Museum under the direction of John Alexander, Ian Kinnes and the late David Clarke. The three ditches on the site have been sampled and produced good stratified collections of Neolithic pottery, axes and flint tools, and the formation of the peat between 5,000 and 3,000 BC is being investigated.

Bronze Age Cambridgeshire 2,000 - 650 BC

General Background
The first people to use metal in Britain are known as the Beaker folk, a remarkable group found over most of western Europe who shared many cultural characteristics. They seemed to be a distinct racial group, tall, large-boned and round-headed in contrast to the small-boned, long-headed Mediterranean-type Neolithic peoples, and they brought many changes with them. These include the custom of single burial, often beneath round barrows and accompanied by grave goods, which suggests a more hierarchical society than do the poorly-equipped family graves of the Neolithic. Their pottery, after which they were named by a nineteenth-century antiquarian, is better made than any other in Britain until the late Iron Age, being thin, hard, well shaped and elaborately decorated. Complete examples, assumed to have contained some sort of drink (hence the name Beaker folk) are usually found with burials.

Metal objects from this earliest period are extremely rare, but good trading contacts were soon established and areas of Britain, particularly Wessex, that were connected with the trade in Irish gold and Cornish tin, became amazingly rich. Grave goods included objects of gold, amber and jet as well as bronze and stone implements, and pottery. Stone working techniques reached their highest point in this phase, before craftsmen seriously turned their attention to metal working, and exquisitely flaked flint daggers, arrow-heads and other tools were produced. Apart from the beakers themselves, artifacts which are distinctive of this period include small and simple flat daggers of bronze, jet and shale buttons, stone "battle-axes", flint knives, daggers and barbed

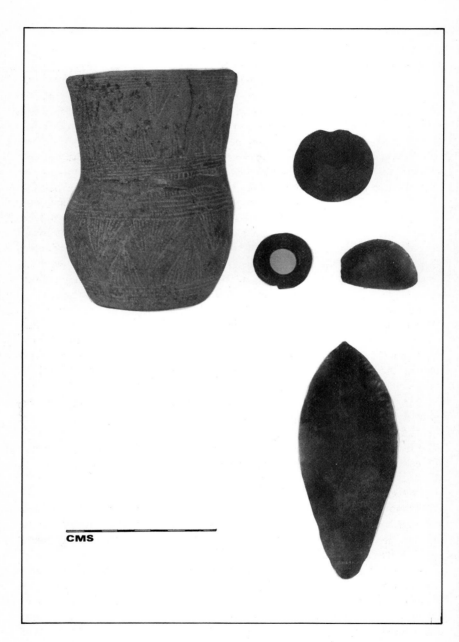

CMS

7. Beaker grave-group from Little Downham, including a finely worked flint dagger and scraper, and a shale ring and button *(photo E. Taylor)*

and tanged arrow-heads.

After a period of initial domination, the Beaker folk seem to merge with the native population and received new ideas and techniques from the Continent. The Early and Middle Bronze Ages are periods of less extreme wealth but with signs of steady improvements in the general standard of living. In particular, well-organized trade-routes made bronze tools available everywhere, which naturally improved agriculture and house-building techniques.

By the Late Bronze Age a number of significant changes in technology, customs and social patterns are evident in the archaeological record. Several sizeable settlement sites are known, with clusters of small, round huts. Bronze was now commonly available and was used wherever it was needed, so the list of implements surviving from this period includes bronze axes of many forms, spear-heads, swords, rapiers, palstaves, shields, scabbard ends, knives, hammers, fish-hooks, gouges, chisels, awls, razors, buttons, tweezers, pins, bodkins, bangles, and rings. Bronze was made and traded by travelling smiths who often had cause to bury their stock, so that we have many hoards of assorted items from this period which teach us much about everyday items, new contacts and the rapidly-changing styles which are so useful for dating other finds and sites. These styles, whether evolved in Britain or brought from Europe tended to spread rapidly and uniformly due to the itinerant nature of the craftsmen involved, the rapidity with which any much used tool of bronze will become ineffectual and the ease with which the valuable bronze can be smelted down and cast into something new and sharp again which would naturally be in the latest fashion.

Many weapons are found, and a large number of hoards are known, suggesting that people buried their goods for safety and failed to return for them; in addition, several hill-forts, a type of monument generally associated with the Iron Age, are proving on excavation to have originated in the Late Bronze Age, all of which indicates a certain restlessness in society.

Settlements
In Cambridgeshire the Bronze Age is in one aspect even more meagre and frustrating than the Neolithic period, for only one possible hut-site has so far been located although a great number of settlement areas are known and at Fengate a large area of such a settlement has been excavated with otherwise very satisfactory results. Our increased knowledge of the Beaker and Early and Middle Bronze Age periods is drawn from the burial sites which, apart from the Beaker examples described below, unfortunately all seem to have been poorly furnished and were generally badly excavated. Most of our hoards belong to the Late Bronze Age, so in this period we have a great deal of information on bronze technology, trade and culture contacts.

When discussing the pattern of Bronze Age occupation we are subject to

CMS

8. Bronze Age bronze equipment. **a.** Sword from Horningsea. **b.** Palstave from Harston. **c.** Rivetted dagger from Chippenham. **d.** Socketed axe from Cambridge. **e.** Axe from Burwell Fen. **f.** Flat axe from Bottisham. **g.** Socketed spear-head from Isleham Fen *(photo E. Taylor)*

the same limitations as when we looked at the Neolithic period, except that we now have a larger number of finds thanks to an increased population and the occurrence of hoards, and we have easily recognizable burial grounds.

The general distribution of occupation debris suggests that the most densely settled areas were those that had been favoured for settlement in the Neolithic period.

In the Late Bronze Age the climate was becoming wetter and there was a certain amount of land subsidence which was to continue in the Iron Age. Not surprisingly, therefore, most of the finds from this date are found on the higher ground, especially in the south of the County and there are even occasionally objects found in the wooded areas. The importance of the southern chalklands, however, is probably exaggerated by the number of finds because the Icknield Way obviously attracted travellers who would be just the sort to deposit hoards and lose their weapons, but the shift away from Fenland areas is clear from the evidence at present available.

Settlements on slight sandy hillocks that were later covered by peat have been excavated at Shippea Hill and Isleham Fen. They were interpreted as merely temporary occupation areas and no structures were discovered. There was a strange site at Swaffham Prior where a workman found a circular trench that contained much occupation debris of Late Bronze Age date and also skeletons.[6]

Beneath round barrow sites at Chippenham there were seven hearths associated with Beaker sherds and flint implements, and on the old ground surface there was charcoal, animal bones and stones cracked by heating, all showing earlier occupation on the sites of the burial mounds. There was also part of a ring of stakes that could well represent a small circular hut like those found elsewhere in England and thought to be the normal Bronze Age dwelling.[7]

The Economy

Agriculture

Farming continued to develop much as it had in the Neolithic, probably with improvements such as the use of animals for ploughing and riding which are difficult to detect in the archaeological record. Certain agricultural processes we can assume were made easier by the use of bronze, and any sort of carpentry, whose importance we tend to forget because it so seldom leaves physical remains, could be far more efficiently undertaken. Some sites do show some change in the relative importance of particular crops, for example, there seems to be more evidence for barley than wheat, and cattle are clearly dominant in some areas at certain times.

The site at Fengate is probably not typical as it is so close to the rich pastures of the fens, but it is the only site in this area for which we have

Cambridgeshire: Major sites and geographical areas.

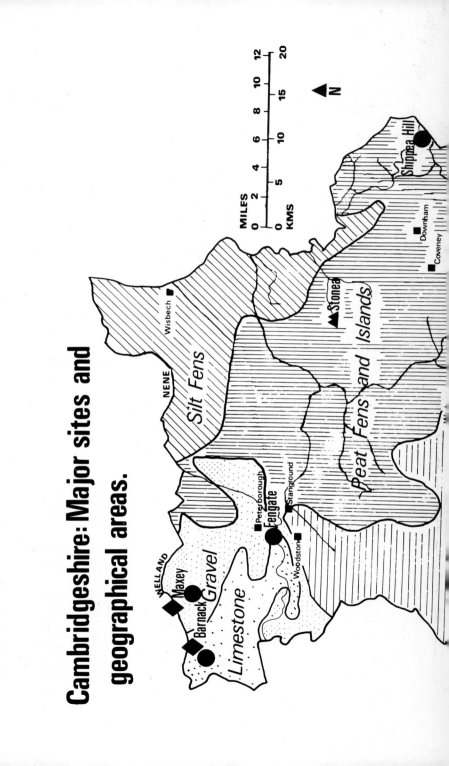

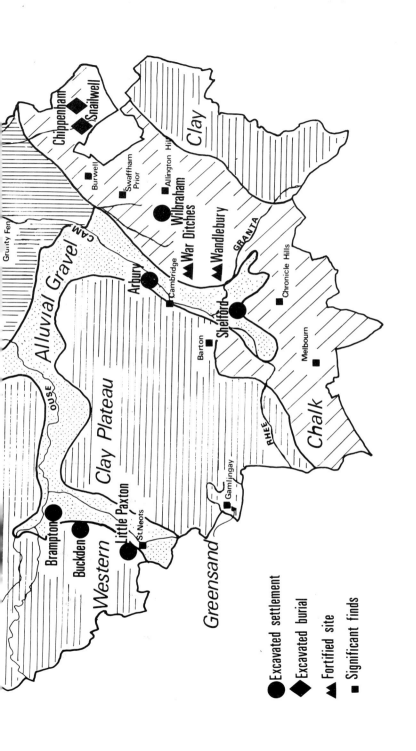

Gruntly Fen

Chippenham
Snailwell

Clay

Burwell
Swaffham Prior
Allington Hill

CAM

Alluvial Gravel

Wilbraham

War Ditches
Wandlebury

GRANTA

Arbury
Cambridge

Chronicle Hills

OUSE

Shelford

Western Clay Plateau

Barton

Melbourn

RHEE

Chalk

Gamlingay

Greensand

Brampton

Buckden

Little Paxton
St Neots

● Excavated settlement
◆ Excavated burial
▲ Fortified site
■ Significant finds

environmental data and details of economic activity. Analysis of the animal bones found during excavations there show that wild cattle and deer were hunted for food but the economy was based on domesticated animals, which included sheep or goats (these are indistinguishable by their skeletons in prehistory), and pigs, but in the main was dependent on cattle-ranching. Some of the bones were of fairly old animals, presumably kept for milk and cheese although there must have been some autumn slaughtering of surplus animals which would provide meat.

Fengate's economy during the Bronze Age appears to have been based on herds of cattle taken down to the fen pastures once they were sufficiently dry in the spring, most of the population 'probably deserting their winter quarters, and then returning in the autumn. The shortage of winter grazing made it necessary to manage the land with ditched and hedged fields and stock-yards. These show up on aerial photographs as a regularly spaced series of paired ditches running at right angles to the fens, still visible for about a third of a mile along the fen-edge, implying both the need and the ability of Bronze Age farmers to organise extensive and unified measures for the control of resources.

Technology

After the Beaker period stone-working techniques deteriorated, although flint is still used for a wide range of everyday implements including arrow-heads, scrapers and cutting edges. The skill of the craftsmen and the pride of the owners obviously went into bronze, which came to be more commonly used as the period progressed.

Many hoards of bronze objects have been found which have been classified according to whether they are 'personal' (presumably buried during a time of threat by wealthy owners who did not live to recover them), 'votive' (left as a ritual offering, usually in an area of deep fen), 'merchants' or 'founders' hoards. These last two types are the most interesting because they often include collections of old broken tools together with newly cast ones in a different fashion, unfinished objects, lumps of metal, moulds for casting and sometimes large numbers of identical weapons. They therefore help not only with the relative dating of types of object but also give clues on manu-facturing and trading patterns — how old objects were collected by smiths, a new specialist group of craftsmen, and were then smelted and re-cast and traded by the same travelling smiths who must have served very wide areas and been in constant contact with the whole range of developing European technologies.

The votive offerings are rare but include our most spectacular Bronze Age finds. At Coveney there was a pair of bronze shields expertly beaten into unusual designs. A third shield was found with a Middle Bronze Age spear in

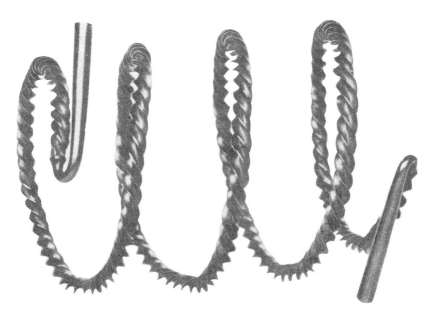

9. Gold torc found in Grunty Fen in 1844 *(first published in CAS, 1907)*

Langwood Fen, Chatteris. From Grunty Fen there have come four hoards but no other finds, suggesting this secluded marshy uninhabitable spot was used for ritual ceremonies. The finds from here include what is probably the most famous object from prehistoric Cambridgeshire: the Grunty Fen torc. This was found in 1844 by a peat-digger who described how, when he lifted a sod of peat the gold coil sprang up with a shower of earth. Above the torc there had been three bronze palstaves of the Middle Bronze Age which fortunately gives us the date of this unique object.[8] Other deposits in this Fen included another torc (now lost), a gold bracelet with 'ring-money' attached, and further bronzes.

Trade

The gold objects demonstrate considerable wealth and far-reaching trading contacts, although, as in the case of Neolithic trade, this contact was probably indirect. Other luxury objects showing trade contacts are the frequent finds of jet beads and buttons from Yorkshire, shale buttons and rings from Kimmeridge in Dorset and an amber bead at Brampton, probably from the Baltic. The bronze work shows that Bronze Age Cambridgeshire was, to quote Cyril Fox, "in the full stream of western European culture".

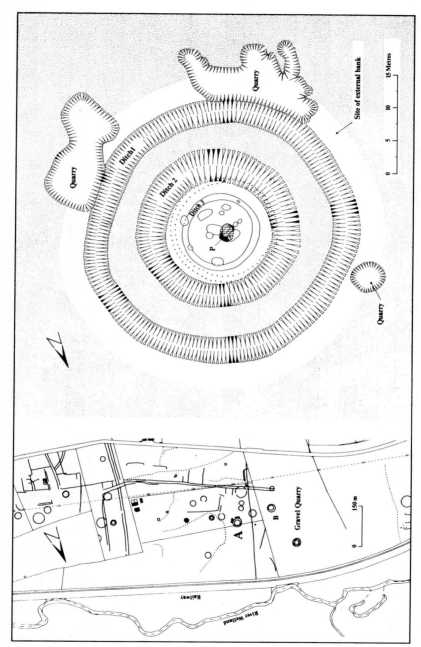

10. Barnack: location of the barrow (A), with other crop-marks, and plan of excavated barrow *(published in Durobrivae 5 and reproduced by kind permission)*

28

Transport

There are records of dug-out canoes being found in the waterlogged clay, beneath the peat fens, and these, as far as we can tell, often seem to date from the Bronze Age, illustrating the means by which people were able to travel and settle freely amid the waterways of the fens and rivers. At Horsey, near Stanground, there was "a very perfect canoe" found in 1828, which was said to contain two barbed fish-spears, two other spears and two forks, which, if the evidence is reliable, gives a good picture of the economic exploitation of the fens. Another canoe, at Chatteris, contained a bronze rapier, which is the only clear dating evidence we have for these constructions. The best recorded canoe was excavated at Warboys in 1909-10 for which we have measured drawings.[9]

The Icknield Way was obviously an important highway by this time, linking Wiltshire to Norfolk and providing cultural interchanges all along its route. Made up tracks were necessary across the boggier parts of the Fens, as we seem to have indications of three causeways giving access to the Isle of Ely. One of them, at New Fordy Farm, was excavated by T C Lethbridge and found to be about six metres wide, absolutely straight and made up of piles 2.5 metres long and mortised beams supporting faggots that were covered by sand and gravel.[10]

Burials

The Beaker folk are usually said to have brought the custom of burials in round-barrows to Britain, but in Cambridgeshire such barrows are extremely rare and most burials found have been in crouched positions in flat shallow graves, accompanied often merely by a pot and perhaps a flint implement but sometimes with more extravagant grave-goods such as those from Downham (plate 7) where there was a finely decorated beaker, conical shale button and pulley-ring, small scraper and a superb flint dagger, and Barnack (described below). Usually the graves are found singly but at Houghton cum Wyton there were two beakers, each with a flint knife, found eight metres apart, and at Springhead Lane, Ely, a sand quarry almost certainly destroyed a Beaker cemetery in the early years of this century, only the latest finds being reported to archaeologists although the workmen described "at least fourteen human jaws" having turned up in the past.

Downham was the richest Beaker group known in Cambridgeshire until 1974 when Peter Donaldson undertook rescue excavations at Barnack for the Nene Valley Research group in advance of gravel excavation.[11] This site had been ploughed flat and so was only visible as a crop-mark but the phases of the original barrow site could be worked out by the ditches, post-holes and burial pits that still remained. The first burial, which belonged to the Beaker period was of the greatest importance. It consisted of a large pit 1.8 metres deep containing a male skeleton with some sort of wooden structure at the bottom. In this pit near the skeleton there was an unusually large beaker, a small bronze dagger, a pendant made of bone or ivory that might be a model of a bow, and an archer's wrist-guard of greenstone that had been polished by careful grinding. This remarkable object had nine perforations in a zig-zag pattern at each end, and these were covered with sheet gold caps. All these objects were presumably made in Britain, but Ian Kinnes of the British Museum emphasises the striking resemblance to styles and techniques of the Rhineland and Bohemia at a similar date.[12]

This burial was covered by a low mound and surrounded by a ditch forty metres in diameter and 1.3 metres deep, with an outer bank. There was also a small internal ditch (Ditch 3) which must have been covered over. The next phase was created by Ditch 2 which was cut between the two previous rings and was probably the memorial for a cremation which was placed in a pit cut into the original burial shaft.

The last phase was constructed with a double circle of stakes driven into the inside edge of the partially silted Ditch 2 which revetted a mound that was partially made of soil from nearby quarry pits. The burial of this phase was another cremation which again was placed in a pit which cut into its predecessor.

There were fourteen other inhumations all lying in a curled-up position covered by this monument, but it was usually difficult to assign them to any particular period. Four were infants, one of which had a beaker, two adults had been buried in coffins, and a man and a woman were buried together with a bone point and some flint tools. The remaining six had no grave-goods or features of interest.

During the Early and Middle Bronze Age most of the burial sites occur as round barrows, generally on high chalk lands, and as ring-ditches on low lying gravel soils, mostly near rivers. The distinction between these two sorts of monument is not important, as round barrows are normally surrounded by quarry ditches and when, as so commonly happens, they are ploughed down, they are visible only as circular crop-marks, while ring-ditches, although by definition only surviving as circular ditches, have been proved by excavation to have originally surrounded broad low mounds. The difference is really one of emphasis and due to geology — a high chalk mound on a hill top catches attention, but in a flat valley such as the Ouse a large ditch is more impressive and easier to build in the loose gravel.

The barrows were intended for one individual, but there is a tradition of secondary burials, that is, of other burials being placed in the old barrow by those whose relatives were unwilling to build a new barrow, especially when space was becoming a limiting factor. Usually these later burials were respectfully cut into the side of the mound, but there are plenty of examples of

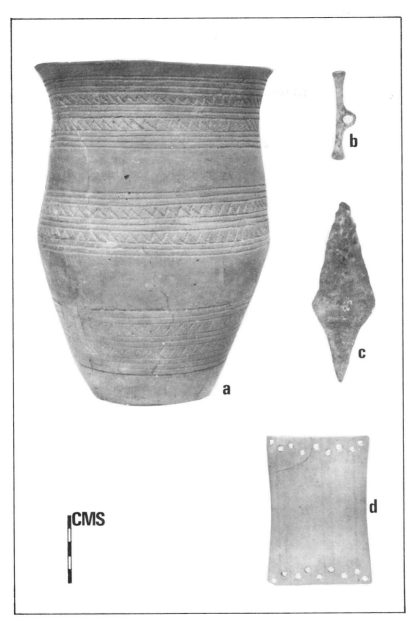

11. Barnack grave-group. **a.** Beaker. **b.** Bone pendant. **c.** Bronze dagger.
d. Greenstone "wrist-guard" with bronze rivets.

31

the original central burials being disturbed and thrown to one side when they wanted to put someone else in. This custom continued into the Anglo-Saxon period, so there are often several bodies found in a round-barrow excavation.

The round barrows which were standing when the first edition of the Ordnance Survey maps were compiled (1836) were concentrated in the south of the County but there were also a surprising number in parts of the fens, the main area being between Mepal, Chatteris, Manea and Stonea. A few of these fenland barrows are still visible as slight rises in ploughed fields, but of course they are spread flatter every year, and in more recent times most upland barrows have been similarly levelled, although especially prominent examples survive such as Goffers Knoll and Grinnel Hill, Melbourn.

The primary burial in a barrow was sometimes laid on the old ground surface and sometimes placed in a central hole. The cremated remains were either placed in an urn, covered by an inverted urn, placed in loose or in a bag of cloth or leather which has since rotted and left no evidence except for the bone or bronze pin which originally secured it. One exception to the general rule of single burials is Mutlow Hill, Great Wilbraham, an unusually large mound sixty-seven feet in diameter and ten to twelve feet high which covered at least eight cremations accompanied by urns, three bronze pins and a necklace of beads of faience, a primitive kind of blue glass.[12]

Information from fenland barrows is very sparse because there was no one in the area who was interested even in trenching them before they were levelled. The only recorded finds therefore are broken sherds from urns brought up by the plough, and a stone axe-hammer from Wimblington. It seems from the fragments remaining that the burials were generally cremations in urns dating to the Middle Bronze Age.

We are fortunate that seven of the barrows at Chippenham have been excavated, five by C S Leaf in the 1930's and two by Edward Martin in 1973. One of C S Leaf's barrows produced two burials, one of which had been disturbed by the plough. The other consisted of a skeleton crouched on its back accompanied by a bronze dagger and stone axe-hammer. Each of these two graves was covered by small heaps of earth derived from neighbouring quarry-holes. They and a horseshoe of post-holes were enclosed by an irregular ditch and outer bank. Another of the barrows covered Beaker hearths and the post-holes of a double ring forming a low palisade, an inner circle of large posts and an assortment of burials.

One of the barrows excavated by Edward Martin was also of particular interest as the mound, still standing 0.9 metres high and thirty metres in diameter, proved to be of natural origin but was used repeatedly for burials because of its suitable shape. There were five graves containing crouched inhumations, three with just one individual, one with two and the other with three or possibly four, each disturbed by the next so they were all very confused. In this grave there was also a bronze cylinder, a small jet or shale bead and the broken sherds of a beaker, which must have accompanied one of the early burials. The excavator comments that this site shows a fusion between a flat Beaker cemetery with barrow building traits and with hints of Neolithic multiple burial practice.

It is evident that these barrows, like nearly all those excavated fully, were considerably more complex than the standard bowl-shaped round barrows and single burials we assume to be the norm, and it is likely that had more sites been investigated to this standard we should know far more about the considerable variety possible in Bronze Age burial monuments.

Ring-ditches are too closely related to round barrows to warrant a separate description, apart from their distribution which lies almost entirely along river valleys. Whatever the limitations of the aerial photography which has revealed these sites it seems that this is a broadly accurate picture and as, unlike most round barrows, they are found near and often covering occupation sites they are a useful indicator of settlements. The only site so far excavated in Cambridgeshire which has proved to be of particular interest was at Brampton where excavations by D A White in 1966 on a cemetery of five ring-ditches disclosed a complex site. The first phase of one of these ring-ditches included a stake-circle around a burial accompanied by a beaker and amber head. The next phase saw the building of another concentric ring and the deposition of a cremation in an urn. There were other presumed burial pits and post-holes within the rings but these could not be excavated due to the conditions insisted on by the owners of the land.[13]

Iron Age Cambridgeshire c.650 BC - 43 AD

The cultural advances and population increases of this period make archaeological sites far more numerous and easy to detect. The best known sites are the hill-forts consisting of multiple massive banks and ditches encircling the tops of hills in commanding positions, which served as refuges and defences. Late in the Iron Age we have a number of lowland "towns" reflecting increasingly organized and centralized ways of life, but hill forts continued in many areas and were the scenes of last ditch stands by the Celtic tribes against the Roman conquest.

During this period even individual farmsteads were often enclosed by banks and ditches and so were some of their fields and paddocks. Few of these can be seen as defensive structures although some element of security would presumably have been desirable but what all these enclosures and demarcation ditches do make clear was the increasing need for land management and visible and proven claims to ownership. This has the great advantage for archaeologists that the ditches show up clearly as cropmarks, and so great expanses of settlements can be plotted from aerial photographs.

In itself this plotting is a very simple process, but unfortunately there are two major problems. Firstly, as has already been pointed out, not all soils show crop-marks equally well and therefore the pattern can never be complete. Secondly, the crop-marks can rarely be differentiated from Romano-British sites without examination on the ground. This is not surprising when we realise the extent to which agricultural practices and ownership survived the political upheaval and cultural innovations of the Roman conquest. To add to our problems, Francis Pryor's work at Fengate has shown that there are even many crop-mark patterns that have been ascribed to the Iron Age or Roman period, but are in fact Neolithic or Bronze Age. Aerial photograph evidence, therefore, has to be treated very critically and to be compared always with our other sources.

The use of iron, which was so much cheaper and more serviceable than bronze, naturally made many farming processes more efficient, and this period also saw other agricultural improvements such as new types of plough and better grains. Population pressures, which had increased from some time in the Bronze Age, were forcing farmers more and more to live in permanent, well-defined homesteads and manage their land as intensively as possible. This is likely to have meant more dependence on arable farming as animal-husbandry always needs more land, although prosperous agriculture always needed a certain number of animals and there is no lack of meat bones on excavated sites.

Increased yields of grain and its importance as a staple food in the Iron Age diet meant that it had to be stored properly to ensure its preservation through the winter. Wherever the subsoil was sufficiently dry, therefore, we find numerous storage-pits which were cleaned out and re-used regularly. Iron Age sites also often produce arrangements of post-holes which are interpreted as granaries and hay-racks. Pits which became "sour" or unnecessary were used as tips for domestic and farmyard rubbish which on a permanent habitation site had to be disposed of hygienically. Where these pits are excavated, therefore, they provide archaeologically significant groups of pottery, bones and metal objects which can usually be dated and are invaluable when looking at many aspects of settlements.

Occasionally square and rectangular houses are known from this period but most are round. The houses ranged greatly in size, from about three metres to about twenty-five in diameter, the larger ones tending to belong to earlier periods and occurring singly or in small groups while the later sites are smaller but in larger settlements. This perhaps points to social changes from self-sufficient extended families to nuclear families with tribal allegiances. Small houses generally were built with a single ring of posts around the walls and a few internal supports sometimes including a central pole. Larger ones might have up to four concentric circles of posts to support the walls and roofs. Eaves-drip gullies were common round all the houses, apparently with the roofs often projecting some way out from the walls to give a dry space for storage, sleeping etc. Internal features of these houses included hearths and ovens, benches, water and storage pits, weaving-looms and partitions.

Settlement

Once again it is the river valleys which are most favoured for settlement although in South Cambridgeshire there are also a number of sites on the chalk lands wherever there is access to water. Due to the higher sea-levels certain areas near and surrounded by the fens became uninhabitable although, however, recent field-work is proving that there were quite a number of stable and prosperous farming settlements even in these areas.

At Fengate, the excavations in 1975 produced what Francis Pryor describes as "the well preserved traces of a hitherto unsuspected Iron Age village". Near Somersham, in Autumn 1976, there was an excavation to examine the crop-marks of a very extensive site for which all the known material was Roman. In the field we concentrated on, however, the farm was entirely Iron Age, just continuing for a short time into the Roman period. Even at the excavation on the Neolithic site at Wilbraham which is partially covered in fenland peat, there is a little evidence of Iron Age occupation in the area and on one part of the site there is a peculiar area which the excavators suggest may be the remains of Iron Age peat cutting.

We know of many sites in the Cam valley that can be termed "settlements" but most had been destroyed, largely by coprolite mining, before it was possible for local antiquarians to notice more than "assorted pits and ditches" or to rescue more than a selection of pottery and animal bones. This occurred at Foxton, Barrington, Hauxton Mill (a very rich and extensive site), Grant-chester, Trumpington, Barton and the Hills Road and Addenbrooke's Hospital sites in Cambridge. It seems that these were generally sizeable settlements, whilst at Abington Pigotts where a site of some twenty acres was destroyed in the nineteenth century there were several hut-circles, much pottery and domestic articles such as bronze pins, weaving combs, querns and a gold coin of Cunobelin (Shakespeare's Cymbeline), a Late Iron Age prince of the Catuvellauni tribe.

In 1975 Dr Alexander, Dr Trump and A J Legge with students from the London Department of Extra-Mural Studies worked on a crop-mark site at Shelford, uncovering a round hut in its rectangular enclosure and associated fields and storage areas which continued in use for much of the Roman period. Using a soil flotation technique some of the seeds which remained in Iron Age layers were retrieved, and these, together with the bone evidence

12. Sarah Lunt's impression of the Iron Age village at Fengate, 1975 *(first published in People of the Dawn, ©Peterborough Standard)*

showed agriculture was based on cattle, wheat, barley and peas.

The Ouse Valley was apparently not so thickly settled as the Cam, Nene and Welland but an increasing number of sites are coming to light, most of them being single farmsteads in small enclosures. Such settlements have been excavated at Alconbury, Buckden and Brampton. At this last site two typical Iron Age huts have been discovered, about seven metres in diameter, with upright wattle and daub walls supported every two metres by posts with roofs resting on two or three central supports.

At Fengate the Iron Age site was better preserved than any of the other sites mentioned, with waterlogged conditions preserving organic remains in several features. More than fifteen round houses were discovered, many drainage ditches, grain-storage pits and wells. One unique find was a "brush-drain" in one very wet place. Such drains are recorded up to the nineteenth century and consisted of bundles of long twigs lying end to end, sometimes covered over with soil.

The houses were circular with walls of wattle and daub and presumably roofs of reed thatch, similar to those of the Bronze Age. The entrances were about a metre wide, marked by the holes for two large wooden posts over which there was probably a covering of skin. Some of the foundation trenches retained traces of the upright posts and fragments of clay were found, still showing the imprints of wattle twigs. The huts were surrounded by shallow eaves-drips, the most easily detectable sign of Iron Age houses.

Arbury Camp, just north of Cambridge, appeared to be a lowland fort similar to War Ditches which is described below, but recent work has shown that is should be described here amongst the undefended sites. The camp consists of a circular bank and ditch about one hundred metres in diameter. Professor McKenny Hughes excavated there a little in 1905 and was able to show that the ditch was very shallow, between one and 1.45 metres deep and eight metres wide at the top, and was almost certainly of Iron Age date. No more work took place on the site until 1969 when Dr Alexander and Dr Trump with extra-mural students from London and Cambridge spent a season excavating there. Unfortunately the evidence that survived was only really interesting for the "negative proof" it offered, with no traces of occupation material in the interior and a bank only one metre high that can never have been defensive. The excavators concluded that although Arbury Camp was considerably larger than most examples and was unusual in surviving to some extent as a visible earthwork, it was probably just an unexceptional Iron Age stock enclosure.[14]

Defensive settlements
Mutilated and degraded as it is, the hill fort of Wandlebury still dominates the Cambridgeshire landscape and is probably the most important of our

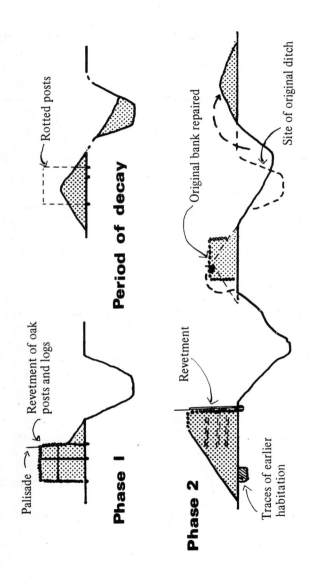

Palisade → Revetment of oak posts and logs

Rotted posts

Period of decay

Phase 1

Revetment

Original bank repaired

Site of original ditch

Traces of earlier habitation

Phase 2

13. Hypothetical reconstruction of the defences at Wandlebury *(adapted from sections published by B R Hartley in CAS L, 1956)*

Iron Age sites. The fort is strategically placed to overlook the Icknield Way and to control movement from there into the Cam valley, but in spite of its height it is fairly easily approached from the east and so the defences had to be built very strongly.

This strength is not evident today because in the eighteenth century Lord Godolphin bought the site for a country retreat and landscaped it. He and his successors filled in one of the two ditches and levelled the two high inner banks, just leaving the partially silted outer ditch in which was laid an ornamental cobble path, and the slight remains of the outermost ditch. The foundations of the mansion, the later stable-blocks and landscape gardening within the fort disturbed much of the interior, thus destroying any archaeological features that existed. At present the hill-fort, which is owned and run as a public park and nature reserve by the Cambridge Preservation Society, is bounded by a circular ditch about three hundred metres in diameter, enclosing some fifteen acres, and still nearly three metres deep. The outer bank is less than two metres high in places and elsewhere is scarcely visible.

In 1955-56 archaeology students from Cambridge under B R Hartley and Prof J G D Clark carried out excavations on the defences and on an area of the interior that seemed likely to be undisturbed.[15] No houses were discovered but permanent occupation is attested by the holes for posts which probably supported corn or hay-drying racks, and a raised granary, storage-pits which contained domestic refuse and human burials and a trench which collected water. The houses must have been grouped elsewhere on the hill-fort and almost certainly have been lost, for a trench cut near the stable-blocks in 1975 proved that the land surface had been disturbed to below the level of the natural chalk. Apart from pottery and bone the domestic debris recovered in the 1955 excavations included iron and bronze pins and brooches, a bronze needle, iron knife and a bone gouge, cheek-piece for a bridle, and some comb fragments.

Occupation of the site seems to have begun in the third century BC when the first fortifications were built. These consisted of a ditch and rampart some three metres high that was revetted by upright timbers, with a small ramp between the bank and ditch. After a while these defences were allowed to fall into a derelict state, the timbers rotted and the bank slumped into the ditch.

The second phase was in the late first century BC or early first century AD. The ditch was re-cut and made wider, the spoil being thrown up to create the low outer bank. The revetments of the original bank were replaced so the bank was upright again, an inner ditch was dug and the soil from this was used for yet another inner bank with upright revetments at the front. From a palisade on top of this inner bank the defenders could see and attack the enemy with sling-shots at almost any point on the defences.

War Ditches

The War Ditches at Cherry Hinton was a fortification similar to Wandlebury, but evidently the site was much less well defended.[16] The fort was first noticed in a chalk quarry in 1893, and since then has been almost entirely destroyed. It is only thanks to the dedication of Prof. McKenny Hughes and Rev. F G Walker at the turn of this century that we have any information at all about this important site. Apparently it was a circular, single-ramparted fort, some 165 metres in diameter, with a ditch about three metres deep. The pottery at the bottom of the ditch is thought to belong to the third to fourth century BC, suggesting a first phase roughly contemporary with Wandlebury, then there was a layer of silting while the site was undefended, and just above this there were mangled skeletons found with rubbish of the first century BC Belgic period. It is thought likely that these were the massacred remains of the last defenders, and it is interesting to compare them with the Wandlebury skeletons described below which were in a similar condition but were buried outside the fort, suggesting that there it was the attackers who lost the battle and suffered the fate intended for the inhabitants. War Ditches was later occupied by the Romans, but not as a fort.

Unfortunately we have no information about the interior of this site, and can only assume that there was the usual enlarged village within its defences.

Stonea

Even by Cambridgeshire standards Stonea is extremely low-lying for a fortified site, at about three metres above sea-level, but of course this gravel 'island' in the fens relies not on a commanding position for its defences, but on the surrounding marshes and wastes. Very little is known about Stonea but its banks and ditches appear to be those of an Iron Age fort, a hoard of silver Iron Age coins was found there, and some very limited excavations and field-walking have produced some Iron Age pottery although there is a predominance of Roman finds. The site was well-preserved in pasture land when the Victoria County History was published in 1948 but since then has been severely degraded by ploughing and levelling and it is unlikely that much further information will be forthcoming.

Technology

The introduction of iron obviously made life easier in a number of ways and made possible greater exploitation of the environment. It was one factor which affected the intensification of farming and iron-tipped tools must have been a great encouragement to the passion for digging ditches around so many fields and farm-yards as well as enabling them to undertake impressive earth-moving operations such as Wandlebury hill-fort. One can assume also that the presence of iron tools meant that nearly every family could have a soundly built house, which is one reason why we have so many more known in this period than in the Neolithic and Bronze Age.

Use of iron as opposed to bronze is significant because it occurs very commonly and therefore it is much cheaper and more easily available, and also that it is more hard-wearing and practical. Its use is also important because it is more difficult to smelt, requiring a much higher temperature, and therefore shows more technological sophistication. Unfortunately even iron was not a metal to be lightly thrown away and objects were generally smelted down and re-cast, which indeed was normal until after the Industrial Revolution and occurs to some extent today, so we do not have a vast number of Iron Age tools, and their state of preservation is usually very poor compared to bronze, and our knowledge about the range of implements is scanty although their effect on the economy is significant. Tool-making again became a local craft and so there is no international trading pattern or exchange of styles and techniques that are typical in the Bronze Age.

The common pottery for most of the Iron Age was coarse, ill-fired and hand-made with simple decorations such as finger-tip impressions and rough scoring, but most sites also yield a certain amount of better-made ware, sometimes either black or red burnished or elaborately decorated. During the first century BC the Belgic influence brought the use of a slow wheel for pottery manufacture along with new Continental styles, and pots were made to a higher standard than had ever before been known in Britain. Shapes included carinated and round-shouldered bowls and pedestalled urns.

Quern stones which occur on occupation sites, are often made from Hertfordshire pudding stone, showing the importance of flour and meal in the diet. Triangular clay loom-weights and bone weaving-combs, sometimes decorated, are often found. The loom-weights are the physical remains of the cloth-weaving industry, but the "weaving-combs", although possibly used for closing the threads on the loom, were more probably used to scrape hairs from skins, for leather must also have been an important material.

Horse riding and charioteering were traditionally important in Celtic society, and Caesar gives us descriptions of how the tribes he faced, when invading Britain in 55 and 54 BC, fought from their chariots although the knives he claims were attached to their wheels have not been attested by any other source. Activities like this leave little trace on the archaeological record, but we do have occasional finds of horse-trappings and chariot-fittings. A fragment of a horse-bit with enamelled roundels was found in Cambridge and a boss from a chariot axle came from Burwell Fen. At Somersham a hoard of five bronze linch-pins was found and from Isleham there came a hoard of eighteen complete and thirty-seven fragments of cast bronze harness-trappings.

Heavy swords seem to be the most popular weapon in this period and one

14. Belgic pottery *(photo E. Taylor)*

42

very fine example was ploughed up in Spring 1976 and taken to the Museum of Archaeology and Ethnology. It was still in its metal sheath and was decorated with curvilinear designs.

Personal adornment was always important and neck-torcs, bracelets, finger-rings, pins and above all brooches, all made of varying metals and decorated according to the wealth of the owners, are extremely common.

Trade

Although life on the farms was obviously simple and self-reliant, occasional stray finds point to a certain magnificence and the princely classes, especially those in contact with Rome, adopted foreign luxuries on a lavish scale. From the Roman world there were imported amphorae that would have arrived filled with wine and oil, finely made shiny red Arretine pottery for best table-ware, and occasional glass and bronze vessels. Amphorae were found at Trumpington and Jesus Lane, Cambridge and there were several complete examples amongst the grave-goods at Snailwell.

These luxuries, according to Strabo, the Greek geographer of the first century BC, were paid for by British exports such as wheat, cattle, gold, silver, iron, hides, slaves and hunting dogs. The efficient farming that is evident in Cambridgeshire shows that this area was easily able to supply such agricultural exports, while the slave-chain with six neck rings found at Barton and now on display in the Museum of Archaeology and Ethnology, illustrates the darker side of trading patterns.

From the second century BC uninscribed coins were in use and from about 30 BC inscribed coins of gold, silver, copper and tin were the currency. This coinage was introduced from the Continent, originating from Macedonia, and the designs used were a barbarized adaptation of classical forms but they were minted in Britain by the Celtic princes and they are extremely useful for giving us the names of ruling princes, their spheres of influence and the boundaries of the tribes in the last years of prehistoric Britain. It is principally from such coins that we can see Cambridgeshire in terms of Icenian, Catuvellaunian and Trinovantian tribes whose borders overlapped, involving considerable conflict in the century preceding the Roman conquest.

Within Britain pottery was traded on a regional basis. Bronze objects and jewellery were the work of highly specialized smiths and craftsmen who probably had personal patrons amongst the aristocracy and their goods are likely to have travelled more as gifts and exchanges than as ordinary sales. Valuable shale bowls from Dorset, fragments of which were found at Barnwell, probably reached Cambridgeshire by such exchanges.

Burials

Iron Age burials are interesting for their great variety and are significant for their reflection of social attitudes rather than any religious ideals.

Very occasionally extremely rich burials occur, either in round barrows or flat graves. Round barrows are generally distinguishable from Bronze Age sites because they have a steeper profile and are found in low-lying ground, but often they cannot be reliably differentiated from Roman mounds by surface appearance. The only description we have of burials from one of these is a very early and unsatisfactory account of the levelling of the barrows near Chronicle Hills, Whittlesford, in 1819. All that is known of the Chronicle Hills themselves is that they contained skeletons and pottery that was probably Iron Age but these neighbouring barrows, levelled at the same time, are said to have revealed two skeletons in each barrow in square pebble-built vaults that were lined with wood and surrounded by circular walls. The finds are all lost but are said to have included a bronze vessel, knife and iron spear-head.

One rich flat grave known was found at Newnham Croft, Cambridge, and another burial was at Snailwell where in 1952 an extremely important chance discovery was made by workmen laying a pipeline which cut through a Belgic grave-pit.[17] The find was promptly reported to the Archaeology and Ethnology Museum and archaeologists led by T C Lethbridge were able to excavate the site rapidly. There was a large wooden construction, probably a couch or bier of which the heavy angle-irons at the corners and iron spikes along the sides remained. The cremated body was in the centre of this construction, perhaps originally in a leather bag of which only the bronze buckle remained. Accompanying goods included decorated bone cheek-pieces for horses, a bronze armlet finished at both ends with beasts' heads with glass eyes, a shield boss, three amphorae, a wine jug, many complete and broken pots and fragments of bronze plating, a bronze bowl, and bronze studs. Piles of bones represented a sucking-pig, a small chicken and joints of beef and ham.

This burial only just precedes the Roman conquest and Lethbridge suggested that it shows all the features of a barbarized funeral banquet. The buried man must have been one of the ruling warrior aristocracy, but apart from his shield and horse-harness his only provisions for the after-life were the pleasures of the table. For fear of vandalism this site had to be excavated in one day and so it is possible that some of the evidence is lost, but it is extremely fortunate that we now have this important group fully displayed in the Museum of Archaeology and Ethnology.

We have hints there were other rich burials; for example, the fire-dogs from Lords' Bridge, Barton, must have been deposited with something similar although the circumstances of its discovery early in the nineteenth century make it impossible to know more, but so far we have no other excavated examples.

Far removed from these splendours are the more common burials of the time. Such burials for the early centuries of the Iron Age are extremely rare and the sites mentioned below seem to belong to the first century BC, before which the deaths of individuals were presumably not considered at all significant. From the first century cremations in urns are fairly common, found singly or in cemeteries and apparently accompanied by no particular ceremonies. While foundations for a bungalow were being laid early in 1976 in Hemingford Grey pot fragments were noticed and Basil Dennis was able to collect some cremated remains and enough fragments to piece together the burial urn. Another simple urned cremation was found during work at Somersham in 1976. This had been cut into a partially silted ditch within the settlement complex.

Less significant still were those who did not receive the rite of cremation and were buried without grave goods. Obviously most of these graves must go unrecognised, but sometimes they will occur on excavations. The skeletons tend to be crouched on their left side and are placed in shallow graves in disused ditches such as the one probable example found at Girton during the 1975 excavation, or in rubbish pits such as those found in the interior of Wandlebury. The great majority of burials like this will never be found, of course, and in any case they are quite undateable except where they occur in a stratified sequence.

Still less regarded were the bodies of enemies who fell in battle, and we have two striking examples of their fate in Cambridgeshire. The skeletons in the ditch at War Ditches have already been mentioned, and a similar discovery was made at Wandlebury during the winter storms early in 1976. The gales knocked over some trees just outside the ring, and a visitor who was walking his dog noticed some bones sticking out of the tree roots. He reported this to the warden who alerted the present writer who managed, during the next few days, to clean and lift the skeletons from the frozen ground.

The uppermost bones had been much disturbed by the growth and sudden ripping out of the tree-roots, but two bodies at the bottom were fairly undisturbed. There was a total of five bodies and it was evident that they had been thrown in one on top of the other with their limbs mutilated and displaced in a shallow and narrow trench, barely covered with soil. No objects were found with them. Bernard Denston examined the bones and reported that they were all adult males and one of them had received a sword cut that sliced off part of his chin bone. It seems likely therefore, that these were warriors who were attacking the hill-fort, for if they were the defenders they are likely to have included women and children, and if the fort were not to continue in use it would have been easier to leave bodies in one of the

15. Skeletons excavated at Wandlebury, 1976 *(photo M. Butler)*

defensive ditches than in a chalk-cut grave. This cemetery seems to be quite extensive, as human bones were noted when the nearby cricket pitch was levelled, but as these had been moved by a bull-dozer little could be said about them, so there are evidently many questions still to be answered about this site.

Conclusion

The conquest by the Romans of most of Britain, starting in 43 AD, brought to a temporary end this steady absorption of new peoples, technologies, styles and ideas which we have briefly looked at in this description of Cambridgeshire throughout the prehistoric period. A new and uniform culture was then introduced, and there are tremendous additions to our sources of archaeological knowledge, which are the subject of the next book in this series: *Roman Cambridgeshire*. Work in our county has already made many contributions to British archaeological knowledge, but the richness of our sites as a complete picture is only being realised now that we have started to investigate large areas on the ground with modern field-working techniques. David Hall, working in the Fens through the winter of 1976-77 is already producing new pictures of prehistoric land-use, and in the County Sites and Monuments Record we are able to bring together all archaeological sources, from aerial photographs to minor flint scatters, and to assess them in their geographical and chronological context.

46

References

1. C. Fox, *Archaeology of the Cambridge Region,* 1923, p.42, 264.
2. F.G. Walker, *Palaeolithic flint implements from Cambridgeshire,* in CAS XVI 1912, p.132.
3. J.G.D. Clark, *Report on recent excavations at Peacock's Farm, Shippea Hill,* in Antiquaries Journal, 1935 XV, p.284.
4. F. Pryor, *Excavations at Fengate, Peterborough, England,* 1974 (Royal Ontario Museum), and *Fengate* in Durobrivae 4, 1976, p.10.
5. G.T. Rudd, *A Neolithic hut and features at Little Paxton, Hunts,* in CAS LXI 1968, p.9.
6. J.G.D. Clark, *A Stone Age Site on Swaffham Prior Farm,* in CAS XII 1930, p.17.
7. C.S. Leaf, *Two Bronze Age sites at Chippenham,* in CAS XXXVI 1935, p.134, XXXIX 1938, p.29.
   E.A. Martin, *The Excavation of two tumuli on Waterhall Farm, Chippenham, Cambs, 1973* in CAS LXVI, 1977, p.1.
8. A. von Hügel, *Some notes on the gold armilla found in Grunty Fen* in CAS XLVIII, 1907, p.96.
9. W.M. Noble, *The Warboys canoe,* in Transactions of the Cambs & Hunts Archaeological Society 3, 1914, p.143.
10. T.C. Lethbridge, *An investigation of the ancient causeway in the fen between Fordy and Little Thetford,* in CAS XXXV, 1934, p.86.
11. P. Donaldson, *A multiple round-barrow at Barnack,* in Durobrivae 4, 1976, p.14.
    I. Kinnes, *The Barnack grave-group,* in Durobrivae 4, 1976, p.16.
12. C. Fox, *Archaeology of the Cambridge Region,* 1923, p.35.
13. D.A. White, *Excavations at Brampton,* in CAS LXII, 1969, p.1.
14. T. McKenny Hughes, *Arbury* in CAS XLII, 1901, p.277, XLVI, 1904, p.211.
15. B.R. Hartley, *The Wandlebury hill-fort excavations* in CAS L, 1956, p.4.
16. T. McKenny Hughes, *The War Ditches near Cherry Hinton* in CAS XLIII, 1901, p.234, XLIV, 1902, p.452.
17. T.C. Lethbridge, *Burial of an Iron Age warrior at Snailwell* in CAS XLVII, 1953, p.25.

CAS=*Proceedings of the Cambridge Antiquarian Society.*

Details of membership in the Society are available from Miss J. Liversidge, 20 Manor Court, Grange Road, Cambridge.

Further Reading

The major reference works are the volumes of the Royal Commission on Historical Monuments dealing with *Huntingdonshire* (1926), *Cambridge* (1955), *West Cambridgeshire* (1969), *Peterborough New Town* (1969), and *North-Eastern Cambridgeshire* (1973); and the Victoria County History volumes devoted to *Northamptonshire* (vols. 1-2, 1902-6), *Huntingdonshire* (vols. 1-3, 1926-36), and *Cambridgeshire* (vols. 1-5, 1958-73).

Durobrivae, an annual review of Nene Valley archaeology, is available from Mrs C. Mackreth, 32 Hall Lane, Werrington, Cambs.

C.C. Taylor's *The Cambridgeshire landscape* (London, 1973) is a valuable county survey. More specialised information on the northern half of the county can be found in M.J. Green's *Prehistoric Peterborough* (Peterborough Museum, 1977), which is a guide catalogue to the Museum's own collections; and F. Pryor's *People of the dawn* (Fengate, 1975).